# GUITAR ACADEMY

**A complete course in guitar for class, individual, or self tuition.**

- **How to read music**
- **Technique/theory**
- **Songs/chords**

- **Improvisation**
- **Ear training**
- **Ensemble**

Visit my online guitar academy at
**www.guitaracademy.co.uk**

### Acknowledgements
Thanks to Andy Parker for his excellent cover design and illustration – *www.andyparker-illustrator.co.uk*
and also to Peter Ware for his very fine line drawings illustrating technique – *www.wareart.co.uk*
I would especially like to thank Gavrilli Nicola for his wise counsel on all matters relating to guitar teaching; Emily Tombs (aged 9) for modeling her left hand in the 'capo' picture on page 11; Stephen Corr for his midi sequencing; Catherine Judge, Jonathan Webster, and Alexandra Mouzouri for their helpful advice; Paul Solomons for his most amusing cartoon of me on page 2; all the anonymous clipart artists whose pictures grace this book; my many students, past and present; and also all my guitar teachers to whom I owe a great deal. They are, in chronological order: Marcus Corr, Bill Lewis, Mrs Bedford, a woman in Hinton St George who's name I've forgotten, George Terry, George Tatham, Chris Ross, Steve Graham, Gilbert Biberian, David Miller, Gordon Crosskey and David Taplin. I hope you're all well, and thanks for everything.

*Page 10: Troika - (c) Copyright 1936 by Hawkes & Son (London) Ltd. Reproduced by permission of Boosey & Hawkes Music Publishers Ltd.*
*Page 42: Morning has Broken. Lyrics by Eleanor Farjeon from 'The Children's Bells', Reproduced by permission of OUP*
*Page 48: The 'Uncle Sam' poster - © Copyright by Schaum Publications, Inc. Mequon, Wisconsin, USA. Used by permission.*
*Posters available at www.schaumpiano.net*

Printed in China

ISBN no. 0-9552749-2-3 (978-0-9552749-2-3)
ISMN no. M 9002118 3 5

© Published by *Academy Music Publications*, 2006
29 Dartmoor Walk, Isle of Dogs, London, E14 9WF. Tel. 020 7537 0148

# Introduction

### To the Student

Well done for making it to Book 2. If you worked all the way through Book 1 you've already learnt a lot – how to read music, playing basic chords, correct technique, tuning your guitar, etc. Book 2 takes you forward by introducing you to 'free stroke', the stroke used most frequently by experienced classical guitarists. Learning free stroke is important in enabling you to play a much wider variety of repertoire, but changing over from playing rest stroke to free stroke can take a little getting used to. It's a bit like the feeling a child gets when first removing the stabilisers on a bike, so don't be surprised if it takes a little time to get your balance – just stay relaxed, practise the exercises, and you'll be fine!

What else have you got to look forward to? Well, there's lots! Great tunes to play, more songs to strum and sing, opportunities to improvise, playing with your friends in ensemble, more ear training, a whole heap of new notes and music theory to learn, and much more besides! So I'd better leave you now to get on with it. I really hope you enjoy learning from this book and look forward to seeing you again in Book 3. Good luck!

### To the Parent/Guardian

Your child has done well to make it to Book 2. Learning the guitar takes time but the rewards are considerable and not limited to music making. Studies have shown that children who learn a musical instrument do better across a broader range of subjects than children who do not. In addition to acquiring purely musical skills and pleasures, studying music improves self-discipline, concentration, and coordination, as well as giving the student opportunities to enhance social skills and feelings of self-esteem.

**Useful website:** The 'BBC - Parents' Music Room Homepage' at www.bbc.co.uk/music/parents is an excellent website that provides information and support for parents of children studying a musical instrument.

### To the Teacher

A reasonable working rest stroke technique is established at quite an early stage, certainly by the time the student has learnt the eight treble notes in first position. At this point it is important to move on to the next stage, i.e. free stroke. A number of popular guitar tutors leave right hand free stroke development until most of the notes in first position have been learnt. By so doing the development of the right hand is effectively put 'on hold'. Guitar Academy avoids this by introducing and developing free stroke, the most important right hand technique, as soon as rest stroke has been consolidated, thus insuring a good continuity in the development of right hand technique.

There seems to be a big divide between tutors for classical guitar, which concentrate on developing technique, music reading and repertoire; and pop, where the focus is on working on chords, song accompaniment and improvisation. Guitar Academy attempts to break down this divide, a divide that many others would also like to see broken down. To quote John Williams, the world's foremost classical guitarist: *'The first part of learning would have to include all the different techniques that other kinds of guitar playing incorporate…learning to play accompaniment, sort of chord bashing if you like.'* John Williams – *Fingerstyle Guitar* mag., May/June 2002.

Guitar Academy provides a whole song supplement to encourage such healthy 'chord bashing' activities. Moreover, it is also the only guitar tutor aimed at children that addresses the important subject of improvisation and ear training. Improvisation comes naturally to children and failing to encourage such a natural and creative impulse seems to me to be a serious shortcoming of the traditional 'classical' approach. Students who are encouraged to improvise from the start do not develop the fear of improvisation that besets and holds back many a classical guitarist. Working on such skills also improves classical guitar playing as the student develops a better musical ear, sense of rhythm, phrasing, and most importantly of all, a stronger musical personality. By combining the most significant elements of the classical and popular traditions this tutor aims to produce not only a good guitarist but also a well-rounded musician.

I hope you enjoy using Guitar Academy. Any teachers or students who wish to contact me can do so through my website at: www.guitaracademy.co.uk – tutor books can also be bought directly from this site, with special discount rates available for teachers and bulk orders.

# Revision Page

Here's a page to remind you of what you learnt in Book 1.

## Notes

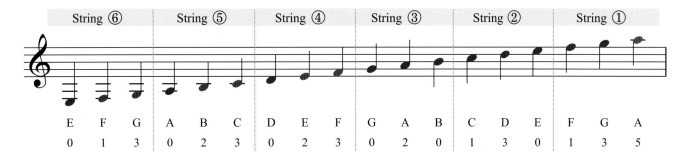

| | | | | | | | | | | | | | | | | | | |
|---|---|---|---|---|---|---|---|---|---|---|---|---|---|---|---|---|---|---|
| E | F | G | A | B | C | D | E | F | G | A | B | C | D | E | F | G | A |
| 0 | 1 | 3 | 0 | 2 | 3 | 0 | 2 | 3 | 0 | 2 | 0 | 1 | 3 | 0 | 1 | 3 | 5 |

The notes shown in blue are the notes you learnt in Book 1. The new notes you'll learn in this book are shown coloured in red [This book will also teach you the sharps (♯) and flats (♭)]

## Rhythms

You also learnt the following basic rhythms.

| Basic Rhythms | | |
|---|---|---|
| **BEATS** | **NAME** | **REST SIGN** |
| ♪ ½ | Quaver | ↱ |
| ♩ 1 | Crotchet | ≀ |
| ♩ 2 | Minim | ▬ |
| ♩. 3 | Dotted Minim | ▬· |
| 𝅝 4 | Semibreve | ▬ |

## Chords

You learnt to play the 10 different chords shown below.

E    Em    A    Am    A7

D    D7    C    G    G7

## ✓ Correct Technique

You were shown how to sit properly and to hold your hands in the correct position.

Posture

It is best to use a footstool

The Left Hand

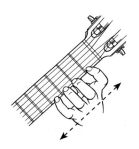

The knuckles should be held at the same angle as the fretboard. Any fingers not being used should hover just above the strings

The Left Hand Thumb

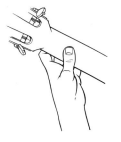

This is the correct position for the thumb – the thumb should be bent backwards

The Right Hand

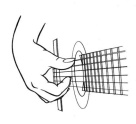

- arched wrist
- high knuckles
- big hole in the hand
- thumb held away from the hand

# Free Stroke

**Free Stroke**, also called **tirando**, is the stroke most frequently used by experienced guitarists. Rest stroke produces a richer, louder tone and is used to add emphasis and bring out scale passages, but free stroke is preferred for general use. It is also essential when playing chords and arpeggios (see next page). The main difference from rest stroke is that in free stroke the finger does not rest but lifts clear of the next string.

## 1. Preparing for free stroke

Rest your right hand thumb on the 6th string and then make a fist in the normal way. Watch the movement of the fingers carefully as they close in towards the palm – this is the natural movement of a good free stroke. See how all the finger joints move together including the knuckle joints, which actually move quite a lot. Notice also that the hand stays still as the fingers close in.

☑ **Correct movement** – a pencil makes a useful prop in showing you the correct finger movement for free stroke.

**1.** Plant your right hand in a 'ready to play' position and then insert a pencil into the hole formed.

**2.** Play the string and follow through to hold the pencil as shown below. Doing this gives your fingers the correct movement for free stroke.

## 2. Playing free stroke

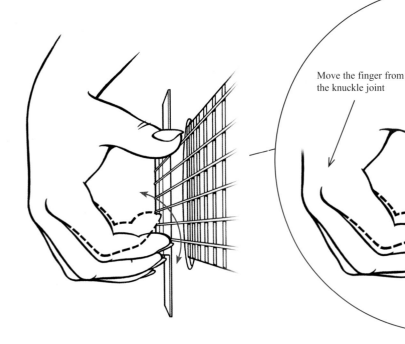

Move the finger from the knuckle joint

4. Having played, the finger should spring back to its original position ready to play again

3. Swing the finger in an arc towards the palm

2. Release the string on the left side of the finger and follow through to clear the next string

1. Push down into the string

The finger movement in free stroke has been compared to that of notching, drawing and firing an arrow, or in the case of the guitar, the sound. Think of the stroke not so much as a pluck, but more of a down-and-in push followed by a release.

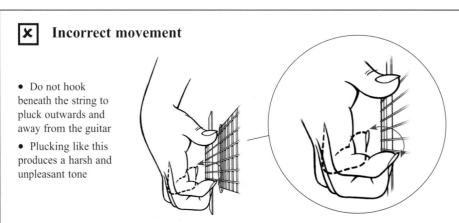

✖ **Incorrect movement**

- Do not hook beneath the string to pluck outwards and away from the guitar
- Plucking like this produces a harsh and unpleasant tone

# Chords and Arpeggios

**1)** A **chord** is the simultaneous sounding of two or more notes. For the guitarist this means playing at least two strings together at the same time. When two or more notes are written on top of each other they are to be played together.

**2)** An **arpeggio** is simply a chord that is broken up into its individual notes, which are then plucked one after the other in a pattern.

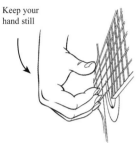

Keep your hand still

**Planting the hand**     Place your right hand on the strings as shown in the picture, so that the thumb rests on a bass string and the fingers rest on strings 1, 2 and 3. This is called **planting** the hand. From this starting position practise Amazing Grace, making sure that the right hand stays still and does not jerk upwards. It is a good idea at first to exaggerate the free stroke movement, bringing your fingers almost completely into the palm to help establish the correct movement. In the end, however, your fingers will need to produce small, controlled, 'piston-like' movements.

**2. Amazing Grace**

Practise Amazing Grace in this order:

**1)** Guitar 1 – with the thumb planted firmly on string 4.
**2)** Guitar 2 – without the small notes shown in brackets (♪),
while fingers *m* and *a* remain planted on strings 1 and 2.
**3)** Optional – Guitar 2 with the small notes included, and also as shown below:

String ④
2nd fret,
2nd finger

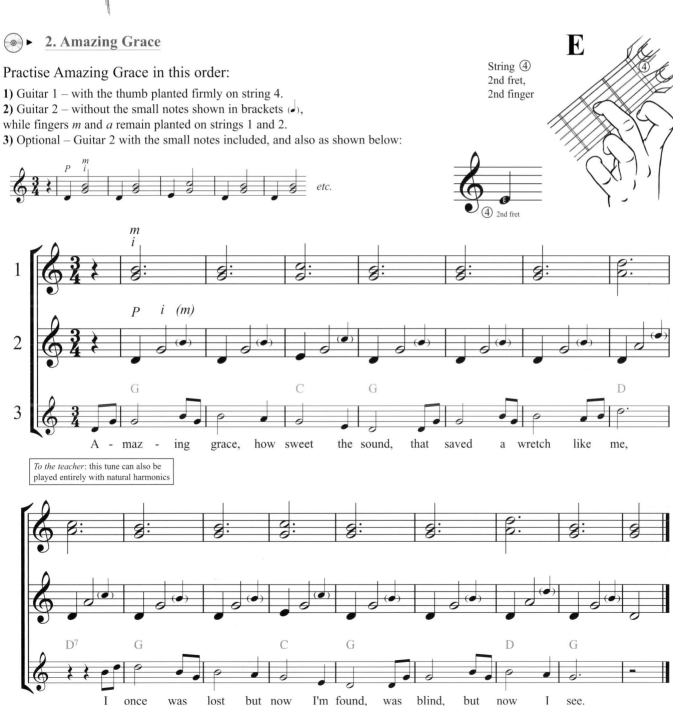

*To the teacher*: this tune can also be played entirely with natural harmonics

A - maz - ing grace, how sweet the sound, that saved a wretch like me,

I once was lost but now I'm found, was blind, but now I see.

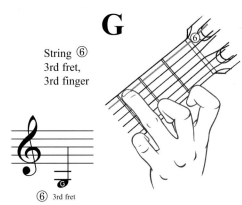

**G**

String ⑥
3rd fret,
3rd finger

⑥ 3rd fret

This ballad tells the true story of the murder of Naomi Wise in Randolph County, North Carolina, in 1808. The song is beautiful but also very simple with only two chords. Sing the song while playing the accompaniment shown in Guitar 2.

[You can come back and play the tune itself when you've learnt a few more bass notes – or find them now using the 'Note Reference' stave on the inside cover]

Guit. 1 (Vocal)
Guit. 2

Oh list - en to my
told___ her to

sto - ry I'll tell you no lies, how John Le - wis did
meet him at A - dam 's spring, he pro - mised her

mur - der poor lit - tle Om - ie Wise. He
mo - ney and o - ther fine things

*Verses* / *Last verse*

*The full story:*

And a fool that she met him at Adam's spring
But no money did he bring her nor brought her fine things,
Go with me little Omie and away we will go,
We'll go and get married and no one will know.
She jumped up behind him and away they did go,
Down to the river where deep waters flow.

John Lewis, John Lewis won't you tell me your mind,
Do you intend to marry me or leave me behind?
Little Omie, little Omie, I'll tell to you my mind,
My mind is to drown you and leave you behind.
Have mercy on my baby and spare me my life,
I'll go home as a beggar and none will be your wife.

He hugged her and kissed her then turned her around,

And pushed her in deep waters where he knew that she would drown.
Then he climbed upon his pony and away he did ride,
As the screams of little Omie went down by his side

'Twas on a Thursday morning and the rain was a-pouring down,
When the people searched for Omie 'cause she could not be found.
Then two boys went a-fishing one fine sunny day,
Saw little Omie's body go floating away,
They threw their nets around her and drew her to the bank,
Her clothes all wet and muddy they laid her on a plank,

And a call for John Lewis to come to that place,
Send him Omie before him that he might see her face.
He made no confession but they carried him to jail,
But no friends or relations would come and give him bail.

6

**4. The Drunken Sailor**    This popular sea shanty can also be played using the same accompaniment and chords, Am and G, as in 'Omie Wise'.

**Verse 1.**
     Am                                        G
What shall we do with the drunken sailor? What shall we do with the drunken sailor?
     Am                                     G       Am
What shall we do with the drunken sailor, Earlye in the morning?

**Chorus.**
     Am                                 G
Wey, hey, and up she rises, Wey, hey, and up she rises,
     Am                                 G       Am
Wey, hey, and up she rises, Earlye in the morning.

**Verse 2.**     Put him in the scuppers with a hose pipe on him (x 3)
                     Earlye in the morning.

**Verse 3.**     Put him in the longboat until he's sober (x 3)
                     Earlye in the morning.

**Verse 4.**     Tie him by the legs in a running bowline (x 3)
                     Earlye in the morning.

**5. Country Dance**

Playing two strings together is excellent for developing the correct free stroke movement.

**6. Study in G**

Carulli was one of the most important guitarists of his time. He was a great virtuoso but also found time to compose 100's of pieces for the instrument. His music is particularly popular with guitarists in the early stages of learning, and his influential guitar method is still in use today.

Fernando Carulli
(1770 - 1841)

The full version of this piece is available on my website; www.guitaracademy.co.uk – under Resources - supplementary repertoire.

# Accidentals

You may have wondered to yourself, 'What are the notes that come in-between those I already know? – say, between C and D, or F and G?' Well, these notes are called **sharps** and **flats**. They are equivalent to the black notes on the piano and come under the general heading of **accidentals** (these notes are shown on the guitar neck diagram – see inside cover).

♯ = **SHARP** – This makes the note 1 fret higher

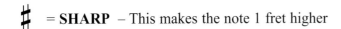 
D♯ is played one fret higher than D – i.e. on the 4th fret.

♭ = **FLAT** – This makes the note 1 fret lower.

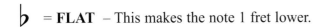 
D♭ is played one fret lower than D – i.e. on the 2nd fret.

**Complete the following by writing in the missing note names and frets – the first one is already done**

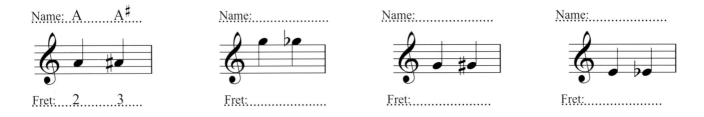

Name: A    A♯          Name:..................          Name:..................          Name:..................

Fret:....2........3.....          Fret:..................          Fret:..................          Fret:..................

Another type of accidental is the **Natural**

♮ = **NATURAL** – This returns the note to its original pitch

Here's the beginning of Beethoven's 'Für Elise'. The natural sign in the second bar cancels out the sharp earlier in the bar.

## 2 Important Rules

**Rule 1** A note altered by an accidental (e.g. G♯) remains altered **at that pitch** for the whole bar unless cancelled out by a natural sign.

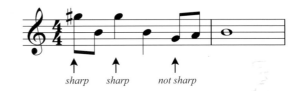
sharp    sharp    not sharp

**Rule 2** An accidental is automatically cancelled out at the beginning of the next bar.

sharp    sharp    not sharp

## Tones and Semitones

A **Semitone** = the distance in pitch between each fret.

A **Tone** = two semitones (or the distance in pitch between two frets).

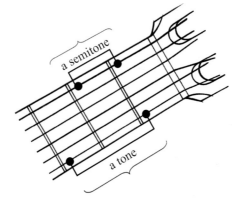

There is only a one fret gap (a semitone) between B-C and E-F. All the other notes: F-G, G-A, A-B and D-E are separated by a two fret gap (a tone), with the sharps/flats coming in-between. This fact will become obvious by studying the neck diagram on the inside cover.

**F**

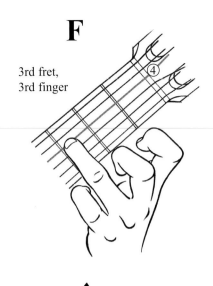

3rd fret,
3rd finger

3rd fret
String ④

### Free Stroke thumb to fingers exercise

This exercise will help prepare you to play pieces where you swap between playing the bass strings with your thumb, and the treble strings with your fingers. Keep either the fingers or thumb planted: When playing with the thumb plant your fingers on the treble strings. As you begin to play with your fingers plant the thumb on string ④.

Don't forget to make a good 'X' separation between the right hand thumb and forefinger, as shown in this picture.

Play free stroke - - - - - - - - - - - - - - →

**B♭**

3rd fret,
String ③
3rd finger

### ◉ ► 7. Hatikva (Hope)

Hatikva is the national anthem of Israel. Play free stroke throughout with the thumb playing the bass strings and the fingers playing the treble strings.

Dm    Gm    Dm    Gm    Dm    A⁷    Dm

### ◉ ► 8. Hava Nagila (Let us rejoice)

**C**

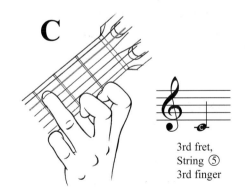

3rd fret,
String ⑤
3rd finger

This tune is formed from the notes of the **Jewish scale** (also called the **Spanish Gypsy scale**). The whole scale is: D E♭ F♯ G A B♭ C D – how about making up your own tune using only the notes of this scale? Make sure you use your 4th finger to finger the F♯s, pressing down with the finger tip while keeping all the finger joints curved.

D    Gm    D    Cm    D

# Key Signatures

This is the **Key Signature**. The F♯ here tells you that all the Fs in the piece are to be F♯, whatever octave they are in; a key signature with one sharp, F♯, is G major. There are 12 possible keys but only one, the key of C, that has no sharps or flats. In all the other keys some notes have to be made sharp/flat.

**9. The G major Scale**     If you play a major scale starting on note G you'll discover that the F has to be made sharp to get the correct 'So, La, **Ti**, Do' sound of the major scale.

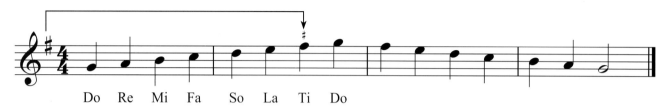

Do  Re  Mi  Fa  So  La  Ti  Do

You can use the same process to find out how many sharps/flats there are in any other key: 1) Choose a key note 2) Work out the sharps/flats needed to play a major scale (Do, Re, Mi, etc.).

**e.g.  The D major Scale**    1) Start on the key note of D   2) Find the sharps/flats needed to play a major scale.

Do  Re  Mi  Fa  So  La  Ti  Do

So, we now know that D major has a key signature of 2 sharps: F♯ and C♯

Most pieces of music tend to stay pretty much in the same key, which means having to make the same sharp/flat adjustments throughout the whole score. Combining all the accidentals of the key within the key signature saves the bother of attaching them to individual notes, as well as making the music look tidier and far easier to read. It also helps in quickly identifying the key of a piece – this is why it is called the 'key signature'! The following table shows the 5 most common keys used in guitar music: C, A, G, E, D – easy to remember, eh?

| C major: No sharps | G major: F♯ | D major: F♯, C♯ | A major: F♯ C♯ G♯ | E major: F♯ C♯ G♯ D♯ |
|---|---|---|---|---|

**10. Troika - Prokofiev (1891-1953)**

Always check the key signature before you begin – here all the Fs must be played as F♯.

**Ostinato accompaniment**

▶ **11. Elegy** ©

An Elegy is a type of mournful composition suitable for playing at funerals or as a tribute to dead people, but don't let that put you off! This Elegy will help develop your free stroke arpeggio technique. Play the piece expressively and bring out the simple melody in the bass. You will add considerably to the moaning and mournful effect if you get a little louder in the middle of each phrase and then let the volume die away at the phrase ends – by doing this you will make the music sound truly miserable!

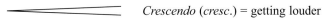

*Crescendo (cresc.)* = getting louder

*Diminuendo (dim.)* = getting quieter

*expressivo (express.)* = play expressively

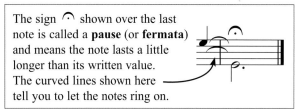

The sign ⌢ shown over the last note is called a **pause** (or **fermata**) and means the note lasts a little longer than its written value. The curved lines shown here tell you to let the notes ring on.

Keep all the bass notes held down for their full duration

✳ See bottom of page

**Using a capo**

*rall. (rallentando)* = gradually getting slower. You often see this sign at the end of a piece of music.

✳ Some of you with smaller fingers may find this three fret stretch rather difficult. One solution, while your fingers are still learning to stretch, is to practise with a capo attached at a higher fret position. The frets become closer together higher up the neck which makes for easier fingering. A basic capo, as shown in the picture, can be bought for just a few pounds – ask at your local music shop.

## A
Open string ⑤

## B
2nd fret,
2nd finger

## C
3rd fret,
3rd finger

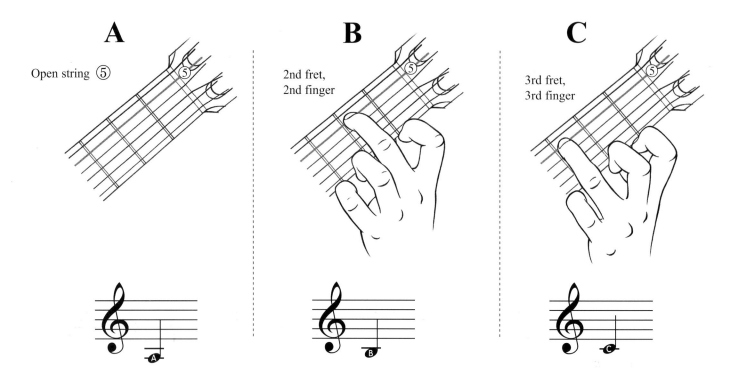

🔘 ▶ **12. Ma Vlast (My Country) – Smetana (1824 - 84)**

You'll notice that this tune is very similar to 'Hatikva' (pg. 9). It has a time signature of $\frac{2}{2}$, which means that there are two minim beats per bar – the 2 at the bottom stands for a minim (or half note) beat. $\frac{2}{2}$ can also be written as ₵ (also called **alla breve** or **cut time**).

*Czechoslovakia*

🔘 ▶ **13. Snake Charmer**

This next piece really bites! If you play it really well a snake will appear from inside your guitar (Honest!). The small notes are optional.

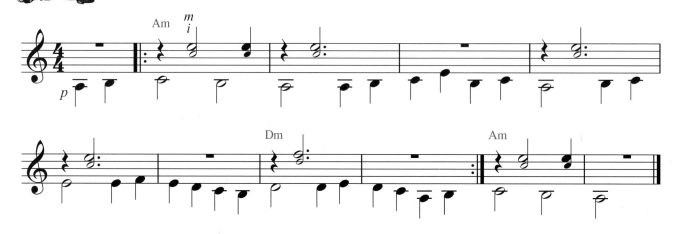

12

# Scales

**14. The Major Scale**

This is the well-known 'Do Re Mi' scale (made famous in the film, 'The Sound of Music'). Practise it using both rest and free stroke.

| i | m | i | m | i | m | i | m | i | m | i | m | i | m | i |
|---|---|---|---|---|---|---|---|---|---|---|---|---|---|---|
| Do | Re | Mi | Fa | So | La | Ti | Do | Ti | La | So | Fa | Mi | Re | Do |

**15. Natural minor Scale (also called the 'Aeolian mode')**

The **Natural minor** scale in Am is said to be the **relative minor** of C major because it shares the same notes, although of course it starts on the note A rather than C. The relative minor always starts on the sixth degree of the major scale; i.e. A is the 6th degree of the C major scale.

# Playing by Ear

Apart from learning music through note reading you should try to figure out tunes 'by ear'. Playing by ear is a very important part of training to be a musician and also great fun! Many experienced musicians are able to play more or less anything they hear – think about that! 'Discovering' a tune by ear requires considerable patience but is well worth the effort. Start on a note and imagine the tune. Ask yourself if the following note is higher or lower and then try to play it. If you're wrong, don't worry – try again! It's a bit like trying to complete a musical jigsaw puzzle. Do you remember the next tune, 'Twinkle, Twinkle Little Star'? You learnt it way back in Book 1. This time it begins on low C, string ⑤. Try to complete it by ear. All the notes of the tune are to be found in the C major scale shown above. When you have successfully completed this tune try to play others 'by ear'.

**16.**

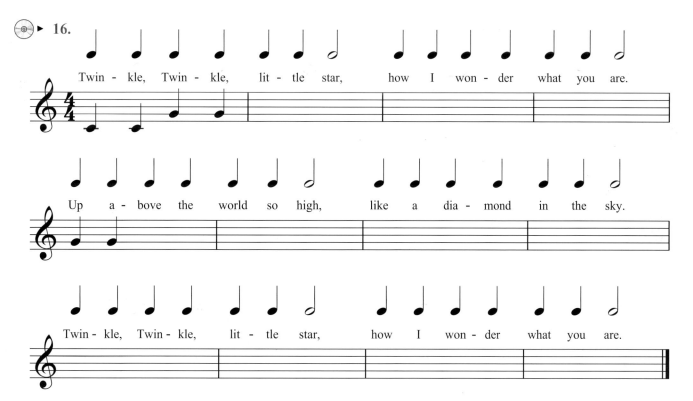

# Ties

**Ties**   A curved line joining two consecutive notes of the same pitch is called a **tie**. Play only the first of the tied notes and let the second note ring on (Although the second note is not played it must be counted).

**Second position** = all the notes between the 2nd and 5th frets – as shown by the bracket.

For 2nd position:
Finger fret 2 with the 1st finger
Fret 3 with the 2nd finger
Fret 4 with the 3rd finger
Fret 5 with the 4th finger

**D major:**  F♯ and C♯

II means play in Second position. Position is shown with Roman Numerals.

**17. Oh, When The Saints**

5th fret, 4th finger

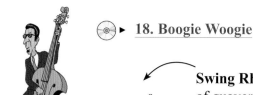

**◉ ► 18. Boogie Woogie**

**Swing Rhythm** – this sign is very common in blues/jazz music and means that pairs of quavers are played in a long-short triplet pattern. The first note of each quaver pair lasts about twice as long as the second to give a swinging 'hump-ty dump-ty' rhythmic feel.

The small grey notes shown below are optional; include them as a musical/technical variation.

**◉ ► 19. The Blues Scale in G**  Here's the Blues scale in G. Beneath the normal music stave is shown a stave of guitar tablature (tablature is explained on page 46). This shows a commonly used left hand fingering for the blues scale.

## Improvisation

**◉ ► 20. The 12 bar blues**  The tune 'Boogie Woogie' is, like most blues music, based on a structure of 12 bars. There are many different variations of the famous 12 bar chord sequence, but the most usual and basic one is shown on the stave below. Try improvising over this sequence using the Blues scale in G.

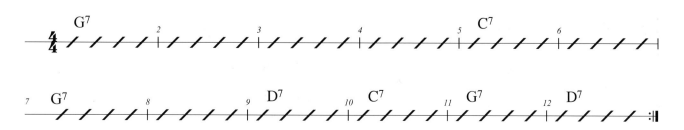

15

**A New Time Signature:** $\frac{6}{8}$ ← 6 beats in every bar

← the 8 at the bottom means that you must count quaver ($^1/_8$ th note) beats.

So $\frac{6}{8}$ = six **Quaver** beats in each bar. ♪ = **1 beat** ♩ = **2 beats** ♩. = **3 beats**

In $\frac{6}{8}$ time the 1st and 4th beats are accented: **1 2 3 4 5 6** Clap the following rhythm:

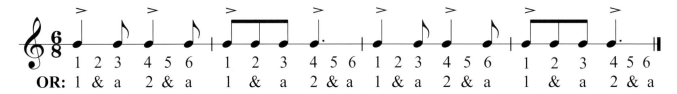

1 2 3  4 5 6  1 2 3  4 5 6  1 2 3  4 5 6  1 2 3  4 5 6
**OR:** 1 & a  2 & a  1 & a  2 & a  1 & a  2 & a  1 & a  2 & a

If you clapped it correctly you should have clapped the rhythm of 'Humpty Dumpty'. Try it again. Do you see?

► **21. Strolling Along** ©

In this piece the tune is played in the bass part with the thumb (shown with the note stems pointing downwards). This can be practised by itself initially so as to give you a better sense of the melody. Take care to ensure that all the notes are kept sounding for their full duration.

Andante = at a walking pace (i.e. at a 'strolling along' tempo).

┌─────────────────────────────┐
│ ----➤ = Keep the note held   │
│ down for its full duration.  │
└─────────────────────────────┘

16

# Improvisation

This optional section requires two guitarists; one to play the accompanying arpeggios, while another improvises tunes over the top using the notes of the A natural minor scale, or the A harmonic minor scale (See 'Guitar Academy, Book 3', for more information on the minor scale).

If you change the G into G♯ this scale turns from the 'natural minor' into the 'harmonic minor' scale.

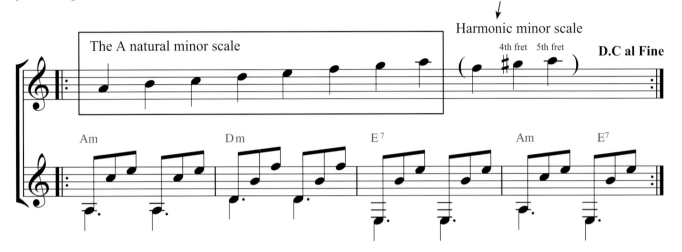

# Dynamics

The different levels of loudness in music are called **Dynamics**. The symbols used to indicate dynamics are explained in the following table.

| *pp* | *p* | *mp* | *mf* | *f* | *ff* |
|------|-----|------|------|-----|------|
| *pianissimo* | *piano* | *mezzo piano* | *mezzo forte* | *forte* | *fortissimo* |
| Very quiet | Quiet | Moderately quiet | Moderately Loud | Loud | Very loud |

## 22. The Music Box ©

I hope you enjoy playing this little study. It is best to play all of the notes on the 3rd fret with your 4th finger – your little pinky! This finger is weaker than the others but using it is very important in developing your left hand technique. It is also important to remember to always hold the thumb away from the fingers to form an 'X shape' separation (see pic.) – moving the right hand thumb into the hand is as bad as a 'spanner in the works' and often leads to mistakes in performance.

'X shape' separation

17

## 23. Heart and Soul

There are two famous piano tunes that you're guaranteed to hear played in every school; 'Chopsticks' is one, and the one on this page, 'Heart and Soul', is the other. It certainly is a catchy tune and I'm sure you'll enjoy playing it. Use the scale of C major, which is shown in notation and also guitar tab. (at position V), to improvise against the accompaniment.

**Improvisation**   **The C major scale**

**D.S.** (del segno) = from the sign (sign = 𝄋 )
**al Coda** = to the Coda – 𝄌 , the last section of music

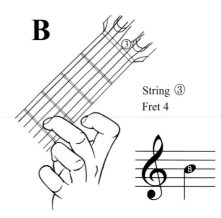

🔘 ► **24. Go to Sleep** ©

I'm afraid to say this lullaby is a little bit soppy, and girly! But on the positive side, it does make a very effective right hand study. The notes with the stems pointing downward are all played with the thumb. The first note of bar 11, B, is played at the 4th fret on string 3; the other Bs in the bar are played in their usual open position.

**B**

String ③
Fret 4

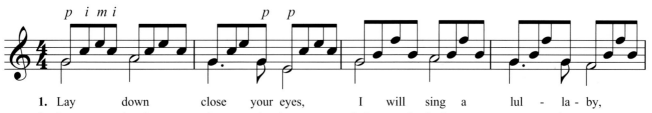

1. Lay    down    close    your eyes,    I    will    sing    a    lul - la - by,
2. Rest    your    head    your    day    is done,    Safe    in bed    my    pre - cious one,

Soft    and    gen - tle    as    you    lie,    Go    to sleep    my    dar - ling.
Dream    sweet    dreams till    mor - ning comes,    Go    to sleep    my    dar - ling.

I    will    watch    o - ver    you,    All    through    the    night,

C

Al - ways    be    there    for    you,    All    of    my    life_

This squiggly arrow means that the notes should be strummed

**Another tune worked out 'by ear'**    Can you think of another tune to work out by ear? If you can, write it down on these empty staves. If not, try one of the pieces that you studied in Book 1: 'Lavenders Blue' (start on C, string 5), 'Morning' (start on G, string 3), or 'Go Tell Aunt Nancy' (start on E, string 4).

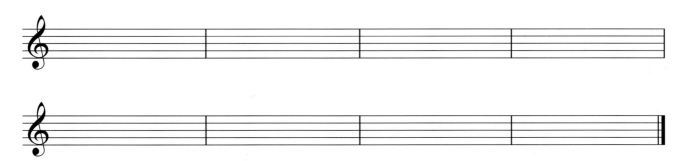

# Playing the thumb and fingers together

It is now time to start playing with the right hand thumb and finger/s together. This is done by plucking the thumb downwards while plucking upwards with the finger in a kind of squeezing together motion. It is quite useful to think of this movement as being similar to that of twisting the top off a bottle.

Make an X shape between the thumb and forefinger

Arch the wrist slightly and keep the knuckles high

Do not let the movement of the thumb and fingers affect the hand. The hand should remain still (i.e. rather as a duck appears still and calm on the water while its feet move quickly just beneath the surface).

1. Keep the thumb straight – do not bend it inwards at the tip joint

2. Do not let the thumb move inside the hand – keep it away from the fingers

Play the fingers in the direction of your wrist

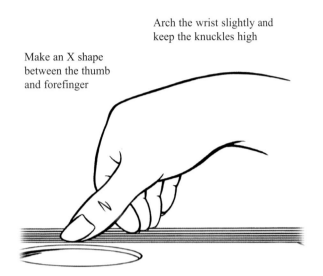

The knuckles should be held high, and almost directly above the finger as it strikes the string

Fingers curled inwards

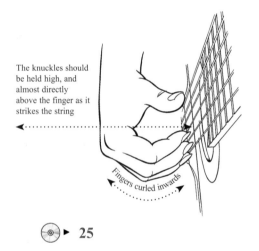

### Avoid straightening the fingers

When the right hand is in the correct 'planted' position there is no need to straighten the fingers or grasp outwards to pluck a string. Rather, the *curled* finger should hover just over the string, play through the string (in an arc) and then spring back to its original curled position. Be especially careful with the index finger which has a tendency to uncurl and drift outwards to make more space for the thumb. Always keep it curled in towards the hand.

⊙ ► 25

## Daily Exercises

1.  <u>'Planted' hand exercise</u>  Play this exercise slowly from the planted hand position. Only two fingers should be playing at any time, with one or two remaining planted on the strings to give the hand stability.

2.  Play **Ex. a** with your thumb while your right hand fingers are 1) planted  2) hanging freely – the hand should remain still even when hanging freely. Then play **Ex. b** – the thumb movement should not change.

20

### 26. Snake Charmer

Here's that snake tune again, but this time played an octave higher with a bass accompaniment. How about getting a friend to play the previous version at the same time?

### 27. Yankee Doodle

In 'Yankee Doodle' you will need to use your left hand 4th finger. This finger is weaker than the others and using it will probably feel a little awkward at first. It is very important that this finger remains curled in close to the fretboard, even when it is not being used.

**Left Hand Finger Numbers**   The numbers 1, 2, 3, 4 written beside the notes tell you which left hand finger to use. A '0' means the string is open.

### 28. Together ©

Notice how the quaver movement in the second line gives this simple tune some variety.

## Correct the Mistakes

Re-write the following piece of music with the mistakes corrected (*hint:* there are two mistakes in every bar). See page 26 for the answer.

# Graphic Score

## Rush Hour!

Make up a piece of music using the following graphic score. As you can see, a graphic score uses various graphic symbols or pictures to indicate musical directions. You have to use your imagination to turn these symbols into music. Select one of the three themes below and use 'Rush Hour' as the main subject. Theme 3 consists of a picture. What kind of music would go with this?

Optional ostinato accompaniment:

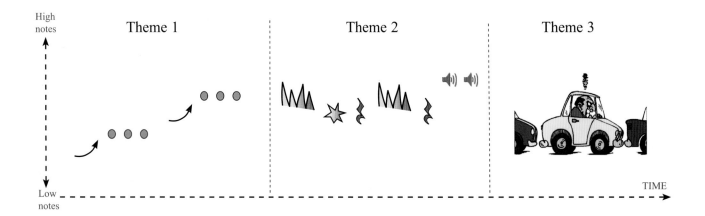

Although fairly easy to begin with this piece gets quite tricky from the second line on. Practise the left hand changes until you can perform the piece with a steady and unbroken rhythm.

◉ ▶ **30. Find the missing notes**   Here's the beginning of 'We Three Kings', this time played on the bass strings. Work out the rest of the tune by ear (the correct rhythm is shown above the stave).

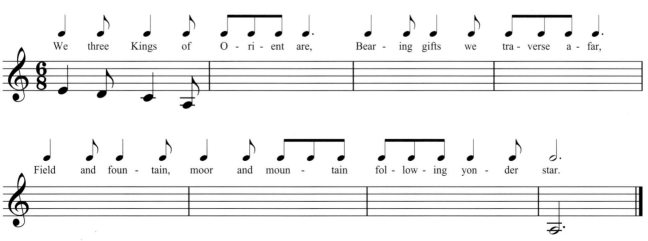

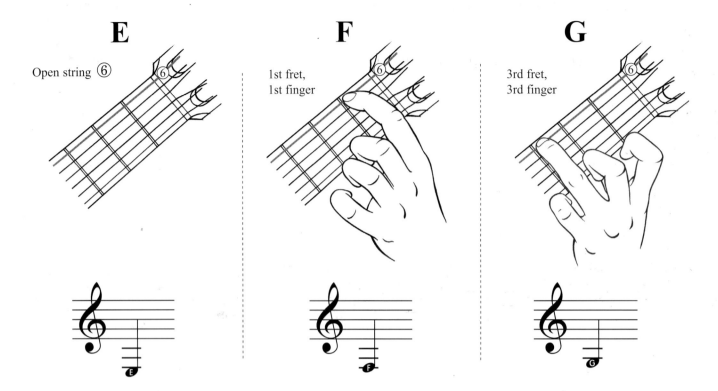

# E
Open string ⑥

# F
1st fret,
1st finger

# G
3rd fret,
3rd finger

### ► 31. Asturias

*Asturias*
SPAIN

This is a simplified arrangement of 'Asturias' by the Spanish composer, Albeniz (1860 - 1909); the name 'Asturias' comes from a region in northern Spain (see map). Begin by learning the tune in the bass. Then practise the warm up exercise, taking special care to ensure that the right hand index finger doesn't point outwards – it needs to remain curled in towards the hand. Finally, play the tune through with the accompanying top E string.

**Warm up exercise**

*etc.*

Practise also with bass strings ④ and ⑥

$$\frac{6}{4} = \text{6 crotchet beats per bar}$$

In this Spanish sounding piece the tune is played in the bass while the right hand fingers play a simple '*i, m*' arpeggio accompaniment. The time signature of $\frac{3+3+2}{8}$ is quite unusual. Such time signatures are called **additive** and show the grouping of the stresses, e.g. i 2 3, i 2 3, i 2. The improvised section gives you the opportunity to improvise with the **phrygian mode**, which is a type of scale closely associated with flamenco music.

**Improvised Section:** Use the notes of the Phrygian mode (+ these higher extension notes)

# The Dotted Crotchet

♩. = **1½ beats** – **a dotted crotchet** (or dotted quarter note)

**Remember:** A dot increases the length of a note by half of its original duration (i.e. 1+ ½ = 1½). From the examples below you will see that a dotted crotchet = a crotchet tied to a quaver (i.e. ex. b = ex. c).

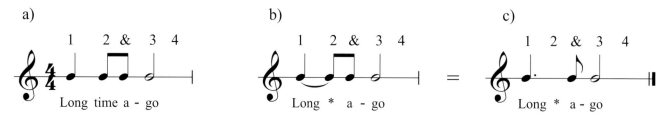

a)                                        b)                                        c)

▶ **33. The National Anthem**

A good example of a well-known tune that features the dotted crotchet is the British National Anthem. This tune is so well known that I have deliberately left 4 bars empty, the idea being that you fill them in yourself as an exercise in ear training – doesn't that sound like fun! If you don't know the tune ask your Mum or Dad to sing it to you. The correct rhythms are shown above the stave so all you have to do is work out the right notes – easy, huh? Remember, your Queen and country expects every student to do their duty!

**Solution to 'Correct the Mistakes' on page 22**     This is the correct answer.

26

**► 34. Auld Lang Syne**

Are you getting the hang of those 'crotted dotchety' things yet? This next tune is sung every New Years' Eve to bring in the new year. Most people can never remember the words (because they're drunk!) so I've included them here as an extra bonus! The accompanying Guitar 2 part is written in the style of a **walking bass**, so called because it keeps up a steady rhythm of moving bass notes, to give a 'walking' effect. You'll find it quite challenging but learning it will certainly improve your reading of the bass notes, and more importantly, it sounds great!

Guit. 1

Should auld ac - quaint - ance be for - got, And ne - ver brought to mind? Should

C   Am⁷   Dm⁷   G⁷   C   C⁷   F

Guit. 2

auld ac - quaint - ance be for - got, and days of Auld Lang Sang? For

C   Am⁷   Dm⁷   G⁷ E⁷   F   G⁷   C   F

Auld___ Lang___ Syne, my friends, for Auld___ Lang___ Syne, We'll

C   Am⁷   Dm⁷   G⁷   F   C   C⁷   F

take a cup o' kind - ness yet, For Auld___ Lang___ Syne.

C   Am⁷   Dm⁷   E⁷   F   G⁷   C

27

**35. Bluesville** ©

This tune will give you an opportunity to practise using the *a* finger and also 3 note '*i m a*' chords. The *a* finger is weaker than *i* and *m* and it may take some time to feel comfortable using it. Aim to produce a firm and strong *a* tone that matches that produced by *i* and *m*.

**D.C. al Coda**

## Improvisation

The first 8 bars of 'Bluesville' provide a good accompaniment for another guitarist to improvise over. The best scale to use for this is the E Blues scale, which is shown below.

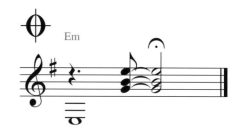

Use the notes of the E blues scale + these higher extension notes

E Blues scale

28

Greensleeves has long been a favourite amongst guitarists. Some say it was written by King Henry VIII who, when he wasn't killing his wives or pulling down monasteries, enjoyed playing the lute (a close relative of the guitar). Whether composed by King Henry VIII or not, Greensleeves was certainly popular in Tudor England (Shakespeare mentions it twice in 'The Merry Wives of Windsor'), and it remains so today.

A - las   my   love ___ you   do   me   wrong _ To   cast   me   off   so dis -

court - eous - ly,   When   I   have   lo - ved   you   so   long ___ De -

light - ing   in ___ your   com - pa - ny.   Green - sleeves   was   all   my

joy ___ And   Green - sleeves   was   my   de - light,   Green - sleeves   was

heart   of   gold ___ And   who   but   my   la - dy   Green - sleeves.

# Test!

Solve the mystery of the following exercise. In it I ask a question. By filling in the blank spaces you will have answered my question, in addition to winning the holiday of a lifetime in Barbados, and £10,000 in cash to spend as you choose. *

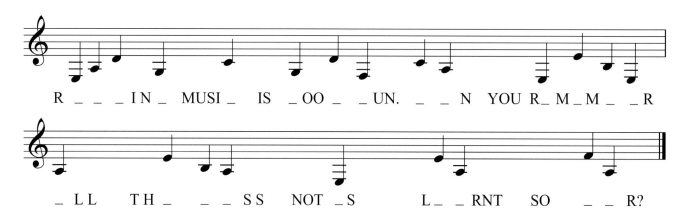

R _ _ _ IN _ MUSI _ IS _ OO _ _UN.  _ _ N YOU R_ M_M_ _ R

_ LL  TH_ _ _ SS  NOT _S  L_ _ RNT  SO  _ _ R?

## Explain the meaning of the following signs and words

𝄾 ...............................................

D.C .............................................

*cresc.* .........................................

⌢ ..............................................

**rallentando** ...............................

⌢ ...............................................

■. ...............................................

*mf* ............................................

$\frac{6}{8}$ .......................................

▱ ...............................................

Write in the notes and letter names in the empty staves provided?

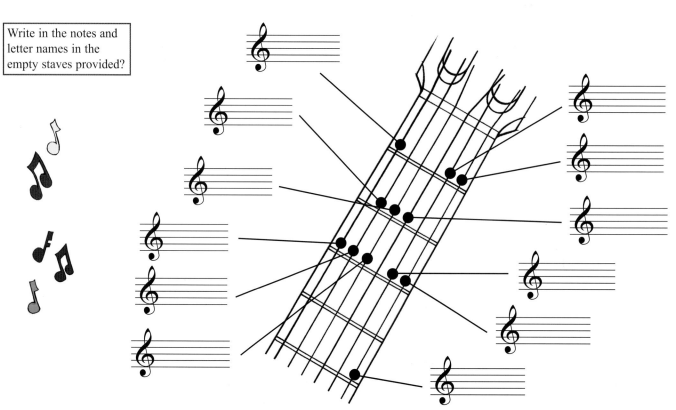

* to be eligible for this prize you must not be older than 18 or have been born after 1987.

# Ear Training

## Intervals within the octave

You were introduced to intervals in Book 1, which included listening tests to identify the various intervals within a major scale up to a perfect 5th. This book gives you the opportunity to develop your listening skills further by learning to recognise all the major scale intervals within an octave. These intervals are shown on the stave below in the key of C.

|  Unison | 2nd (major) | 3rd (major) | 4th (perfect) | 5th (perfect) | 6th (major) | 7th (major) | Octave |
|---|---|---|---|---|---|---|---|

### ▶ 37   Practising interval recognition

The following table provides examples of well known songs for all the intervals within a major scale (I don't actually know a well known song that begins with a major 7th [let me know if you do!], but you can use the 1st and 3rd notes of 'Somewhere over the Rainbow'). Using this table as a guide, try to identify the intervals on the CD – the answers are given at the bottom of page 45.

| | C ➜ ? | INTERVAL NAME | SONG EXAMPLES |
|---|---|---|---|
| DO | C ➜ C | Unison | Jingle Bells; One Man went to Mow |
| RE | C ➜ D | Major 2nd | Frére Jacques; Happy Birthday; EastEnders |
| MI | C ➜ E | Major 3rd | Kumbaya; Morning Has Broken |
| FA | C ➜ F | Perfect 4th | Away in a Manger; Shalom Chaverim; Amazing Grace |
| SO | C ➜ G | Perfect 5th | Twinkle, Twinkle Little Star; Lavenders Blue |
| LA | C ➜ A | Major 6th | My Bonnie; The Lord's My Shepherd; My Way |
| TI | C ➜ B | Major 7th | Somewhere Over The Rainbow (1st and 3rd note). |
| DO | C ➜ C | Octave | Somewhere Over The Rainbow; Bali Ha'i |

**Interval Mnemonics**

### ▶ 49   Major or Dominant 7th chord?

**Major chords** are the chords that are called just C, or D, or G etc, and have nothing more added to the name, such as, for example, 'm' – minor (Cm, Dm, Gm), or '7' (C7, D7, G7). Major chords sound happy and restful. **Dominant 7th chords** are those chords which go by the name of C7, G7, D7 etc. Dominant 7th chords always sound more tense and restless when compared to major chords, as if they need to change or 'resolve' to another chord. They also have quite a 'bluesy' and 'funky' sound.

Listen to the examples on the CD and decide which chord is major and which dominant 7th – the more you practise these exercises the quicker you will become at recognising the different sounds of these chords.

## Useful Ear training websites

www.good-ear.com   This site provides many different types of ear-training exercises.

www.musictheory.net   Go to the 'Interval Ear Trainer' to practise your intervals. You can choose to download the whole site if you want (at just 4.9 MB) and practise the exercises offline.

# Injuns!©

Have heap big fun playing this tune! On repeating the tune from the D.S sign, guitar 1 can play an octave higher (*8va*) – as played on the CD.
D.S. (del segno) = from the sign (sign = 𝄋 )

♩ = 80

**Improvised Section:** Use the notes of the Em pentatonic scale (+ the high G).

Em pentatonic scale

**D.S al Coda**
( *8va* on repeat
= octave higher )

# Easy and Sleazy! ©

I hope you enjoy playing this 'easy' and 'sleazy' piece. As is usual
with Blues/Jazz music, the quaver rhythms should be 'swung' so that
pairs of quavers are played in a long-short triplet pattern.

Swing or 'swung' rhythms are usually notated thus:

There are also optional percussive taps on beats 2 and 4. This could be:
1) Finger clicks.
2) Striking the strings with the back of the right hand fingernails.
Make use of the blues scale in the improvised section and have fun
making up your own tunes and rhythms.

Optional Percussion throughout

**Improvised Section:**

+ these 2 notes

The E Blues scale

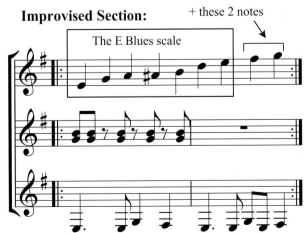

# Cool Cat Blues ©

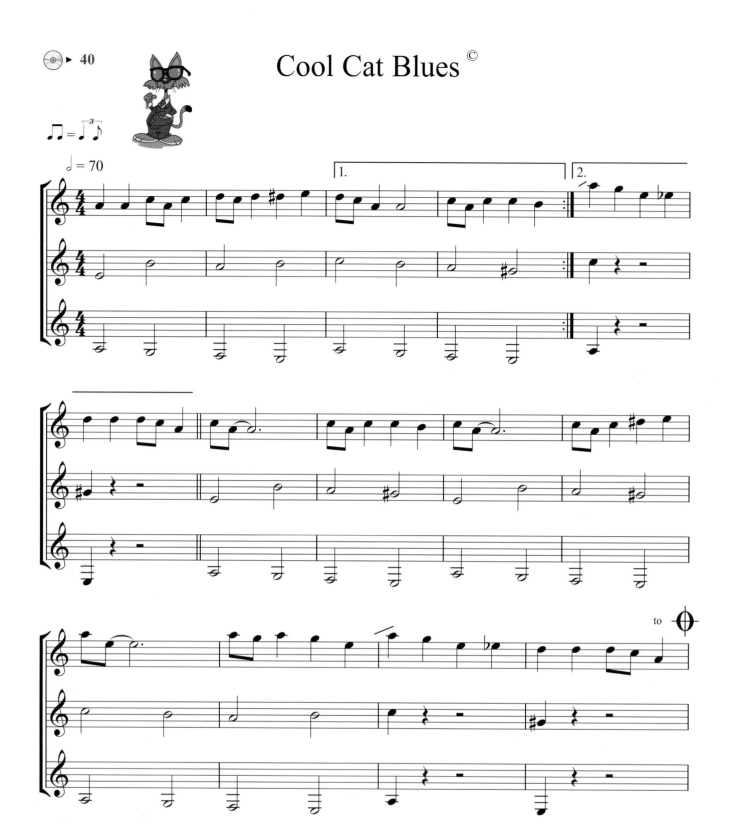

**Improvised Section:** Just play any old thing that comes into your head man! (use the blues scale). Swap the parts so that all the players get to improvise. Then repeat the main tune above and end with this bar.

A Blues scale

D.C al Coda

# Long, Long Ago

# Olé!

 ▶ 42

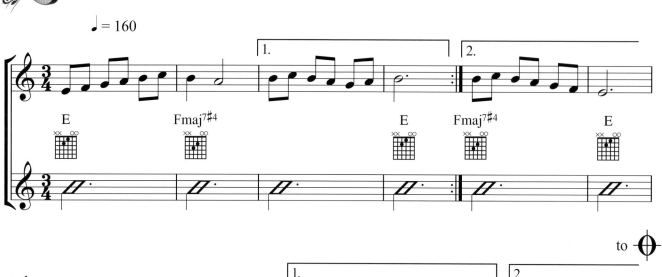

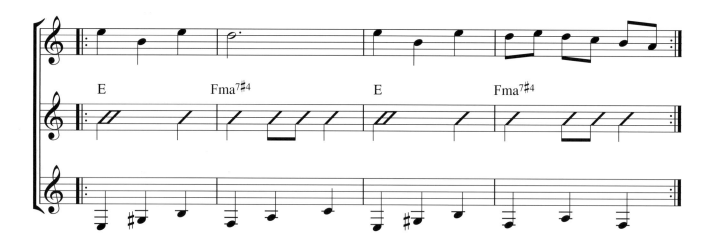

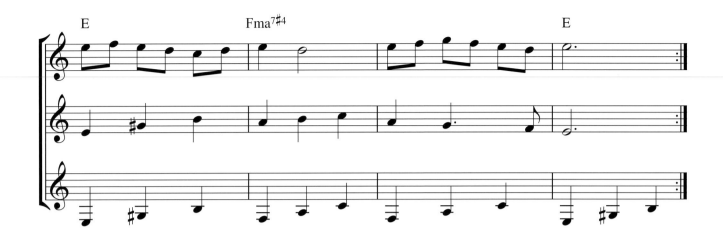

**Improvised Section:** Use the E Phrygian scale (+ the higher extention notes)

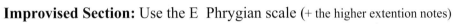

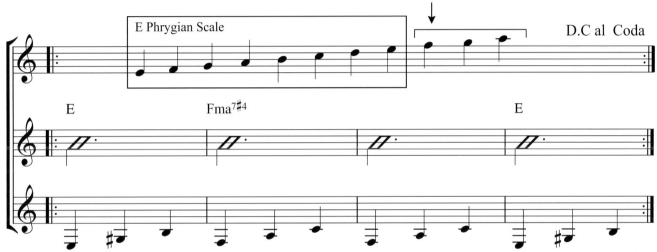

 **43**

# Pavane

Arbeau
(1520-1595)

The **Pavane** was a stately court dance of the 16th and early 17th centuries that was often used as an introductory, processional dance. This piece sounds very effective with an accompanying rhythm played either on the tambourine, or by tapping the back of the guitar.

There is also a new note in guitar 1: – a high B to be played on string ①, fret 7.

Optional Percussion throughout

# This Train

This popular gospel song has been recorded by many artists, including Johnny Cash and Bob Marley. All the chords are quite easy except for B7 which is, quite literally, a bit of a handful! The suggested strumming rhythm will give you a good basic train chugging rhythm. You may like to vary this in the gaps between the singing by creating your own strumming patterns.

Strumming rhythm:

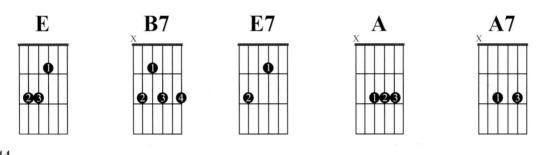

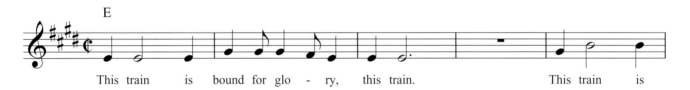

This train    is    bound for glo - ry,    this train.                    This train    is

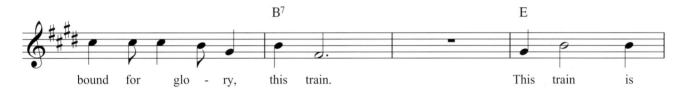

bound    for    glo - ry,    this train.                    This    train    is

bound    for    glo - ry,    don't ride    no - thin' but the    right - eous and the ho - ly!

This    train    is    bound    for    glo - ry,    this    train.

*Verse 2:*
This train don't carry no gamblers, this train *(x2)*
This train don't carry no gamblers
No midnight ramblers, no bar fliers!
This train is bound for glory, this train.

*Verse 3:*
This train don't carry no liars, this train *(x2)*
This train don't carry no liars
No hypocrites, no bar liars!
This train is bound for glory, this train.

*Verse 4:*
This train don't carry black or white, this train *(x2)*
This train don't carry black or white,
Everybody's treated all alike!
This train is bound for glory, this train.

# Jamaica Farewell

You'll need to learn a calypso strum to do justice to this lively West Indian folk song. This has a syncopated rhythm with the pattern of stresses being **1** 2 3, **1** 2 3, **1** 2. **Syncopation** is the name given to a rhythm where the accents are shifted and come in unexpected places. For example, in the first strumming rhythm you don't strum on the third beat as you might expect. This syncopation has the effect of 'jazzing up' the rhythm and making the song swing. The second calypso rhythm is less common and rather tricky, but is included here as an interesting variation that you might like to try.

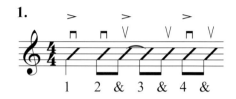

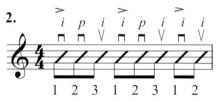

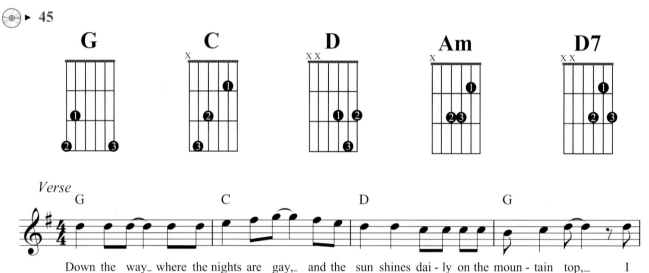

Down the way_ where the nights are gay,_ and the sun shines dai - ly on the moun - tain top,_ I took a trip_ on a sail - ing ship,_ and when I reached Ja - mai - ca I made a stop. But I'm

sad to say_ that I'm on my way,_ won't be back, for man - y a day._ My heart is down my head is turn - ing a - round I had to leave a little girl in King - ston Town

*Verse 2:*
Down in the market you can hear
Ladies cry out as on their heads they bear
Akkai rice, salt fish are nice
And the rum is fine any time of year.
*Chorus*

*Verse 3:*
Sounds of laughter everywhere
And the dancing girls swing to and fro'.
I must admit my heart is there
Though I've been from Maine to Mexico.
*Chorus*

# House of the Rising Sun

Finger-picking style: use the same style as for 'Scarborough Fair'.

Strumming rhythm

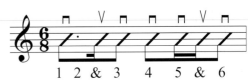

1 2 & 3   4 5 & 6

This song is shown in two keys: Am and also Em. Try it in both – the chords for the key of Em are all shown in brackets. One advantage of playing it in Em is that you miss out the tricky F chord.

Try this version of F if the other one's too difficult

*Verse 2:*
My mother was a tailor
She sewed my new blue jeans
And my father was a gamblin' man
Down in New Orleans

*Verse 3:*
Now the only thing a gambler needs
Is a suitcase and a trunk
And the only time he's satisfied
Is when he's all a-drunk

*Verse 4:*
With one foot on the platform
And the other on the train
I'm goin' back to New Orleans
To wear that ball and chain

*Verse 5:*
Now mothers tell your children
Not to do as I have done
And spend your life in pain and misery
In the House of the Rising Sun

# Morning Has Broken

Lyrics: Eleanor Farjeon

This song, derived from a traditional Welsh tune, became a big hit for Cat Stevens in 1971. The fingerpicking accompaniment is quite challenging: Begin the pattern with the thumb playing the bass note of each chord. The fingers then pluck the same string pattern throughout, as shown within the enclosed brackets. If you find this too difficult play the same accompaniment as in Scarborough Fair.

Finger-picking style:

Strumming rhythm:

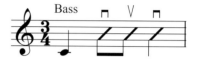

**Bass Strum style:** Pluck the bass note of each chord before strumming the rest of the pattern.

C    Am    Dm    G    F    Em    D7    G7    D

► 47

Mor - ning has bro - ken, like the first mor - ning,

Black - bird has spo - ken like the first bird.

Praise for the sing - ing, praise for the mor - ning,

praise for them spring - ing, fresh from the world.

*Verse 2:*
Sweet the rain's new fall, sunlit from heaven,
Like the first dew fall on the first grass,
Praise for the sweetness of the wet garden
Sprung in completeness, where his feet pass.

*Verse 3:*
Mine is the sunlight, mine is the morning
Born of the one light, Eden saw play.
Praise with elation, praise every morning
God's recreation of the new day.

# The Sloop John B.

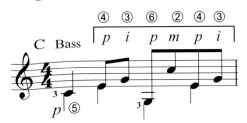

Here's another traditional calypso song. The suggested fingerpicking style is called **Alternating bass** (or 'Travis style'). The pattern remains the same throughout except for Dm and F where the string sequence is: Bass (4), 3, 2, 4, 1, 3, 2.

**Strumming rhythm:**

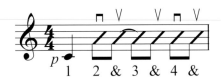

This is a calypso rhythm, which begins with the thumb playing the bass note.

**Finger-picking style:**

| C | G | G7 | C7 | F | Dm |
|---|---|---|---|---|---|
| 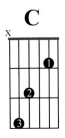 |  | 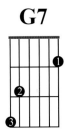 | 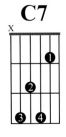 | 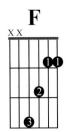 |  |

48

We came on the Sloop John B., my grand pap-py and me.

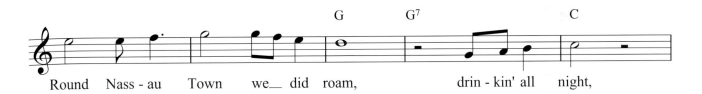

Round Nass-au Town we did roam, drin-kin' all night,

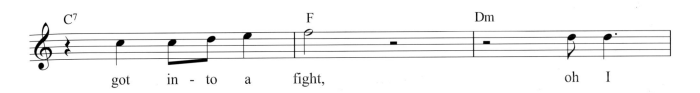

got in-to a fight, oh I

feel so broke up, I wan-na go home.

*Chorus*
So hoist up the John B. sails
See how the mainsails set
Send for the captain ashore
Let me go home, let me go home,
Let me go home, I feel so broke up
I wanna go home

*Verse 2:*
The first mate he got drunk
Broke up the people's trunk
Constable had to come and take him away
Sheriff Johnstone, please let me alone
I feel so broke up
I wanna go home.
*Chorus.*

# Chord Theory

## Scales and Keys

Nearly all the music you hear is based on scales. Remember the C major and A minor scales you learnt on page 13? On the same page was an exercise where you wrote down the notes for 'Twinkle, Twinkle, Little Star'. Well, all of the notes of that tune come from the C major scale (check it out if you don't believe me!). For this reason the tune is said to be in the key of C major. A **Key** in music is like a family made up of all of the notes of the scale. There are major keys and also minor keys although most music is written in a major key.

## Primary Chords – I, IV and V

The most important chords in any key are the **Primary Chords**. These are the chords with the same letter name as the 1st, 4th and 5th degrees of the scale. Music theorists prefer using roman numerals to normal everyday numbers so instead of 1, 4 and 5 we use I, IV and V. In the key of C major this would give us the primary chords of C, F and G, as shown in the following table.

| Scale degree | I | II | III | IV | V | VI | VII | VIII |
|---|---|---|---|---|---|---|---|---|
| Note name | C | D | E | F | G | A | B | C |
| '3 Chord Trick' harmony – see below | C | G | C | F | C or G | F | G | C |

## The 'Three Chord Trick'

The table above shows how all of the notes of the major scale can be harmonised using only the three primary chords. Most songs, even those that have quite a sophisticated harmony, can be simplified to just three primary chords. This is known as the 'Three Chord Trick'.

## Transposition

Finding the primary chords in any key is easy. It's simply a question of starting on the key or root note and counting up the scale tones until you get to IV and V, the notes on which the chords are built. Here's a table showing you the primary chords in the five most common guitar keys: C, A, G, E, D.

| KEY | I | IV | V |
|---|---|---|---|
| Key of C | C | F | G |
| Key of A | A | D | E |
| Key of G | G | C | D |
| Key of E | E | A | B |
| Key of D | D | G | A |

In any key the chords I, IV and V have the same relationship with each other: In the key of A these chords are A (I), D (IV) and E (V), the same chords used to play 'Kumbaya'; but in the key of C these primary chords become C (I), F (IV) and G (V). So, if you want to play Kumbaya in the key of C you need the chords: C, F and G. When you play a piece of music in a different key it is called **Transposition**.

### Transpose Kumbaya into the keys of C, G, D and E

```
              I                IV  I                    IV  V
Key of A:     A                D   A                    D   E
              Kumbaya my Lord, Kumbaya.  Kumbaya my Lord, Kumbaya.
```

| | | | |
|---|---|---|---|
| **Key of C:** | C | ☐ ☐ | ☐ ☐ |

Kumbaya my Lord, Kumbaya.  Kumbaya my Lord, Kumbaya.

| | | | |
|---|---|---|---|
| **Key of G:** | G | ☐ ☐ | ☐ ☐ |

Kumbaya my Lord, Kumbaya.  Kumbaya my Lord, Kumbaya.

| | | | |
|---|---|---|---|
| **Key of D:** | D | ☐ ☐ | ☐ ☐ |

Kumbaya my Lord, Kumbaya.  Kumbaya my Lord, Kumbaya.

| | | | |
|---|---|---|---|
| **Key of E:** | E | ☐ ☐ | ☐ B7 |

Kumbaya my Lord, Kumbaya.  Kumbaya my Lord, Kumbaya.

> There are many situations when a musician needs to **transpose**. For example, a piece of music may be written in a key that is too high or low to sing. The answer is to transpose it into a key that is more suited to the singer.

> In the key of E, chord V is B. This chord is very difficult so play B7 instead – it will sound perfectly fine!

# Chord Test!

With the new chords studied in this book you should now know a total of 15 different chords. Here's a test to see how well you remember them. Write in the left hand fingerings and don't forget to put an X over the strings that don't sound.

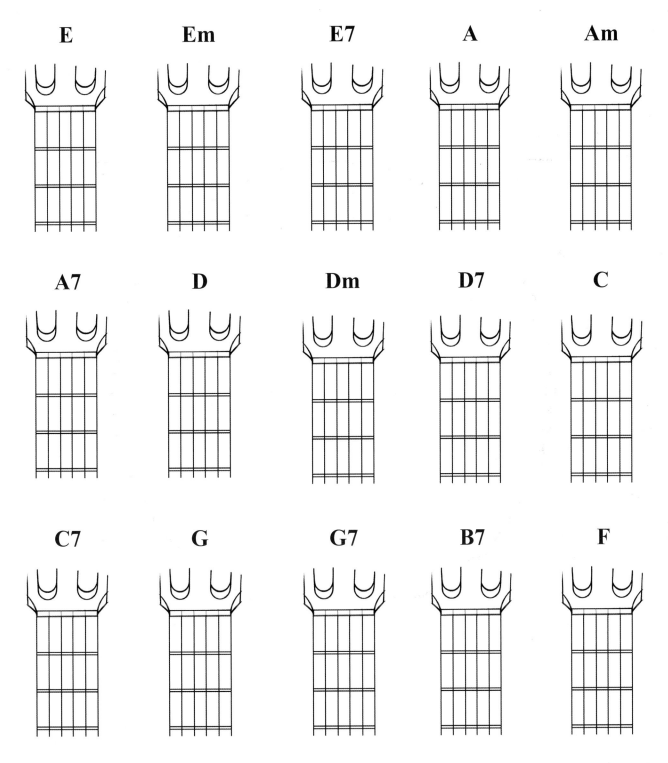

⊙ ► 37  Answers to the interval tests on page 31

⊙ ► 49  Answers to the chord recognition tests on page 31

| | | | |
|---|---|---|---|
| 1) maj. 2nd | 6) maj. 6th | 11) perf. 5th | 16) maj. 3rd |
| 2) perf. 4th | 7) maj. 2nd | 12) maj. 2nd | 17) perf. 5th |
| 3) perf. 5th | 8) maj. 7th | 13) octave | 18) perf. 4th |
| 4) maj. 3rd | 9) maj. 3rd | 14) maj. 7th | 19) maj. 7th |
| 5) octave | 10) perf. 4th | 15) maj. 6th | 20) octave |

| | |
|---|---|
| 1) maj/dom7th (A  A7) | 6) dom7th/maj (D7  D) |
| 2) maj/dom7th (D  D7) | 7) maj/dom7th (A  A7) |
| 3) dom7th/maj (G7  G) | 8) maj/dom7th (C  C7) |
| 4) dom7th/maj (C7  C) | 9) dom7th/maj (E7  E) |
| 5) maj/dom7th (E  E7) | 10) maj/dom7th (G  G7) |

# The Guitar and the Internet

There are a great variety of useful websites for the guitarist devoted to helping you play better. The internet can be particularly helpful when looking for the chords to your favourite songs. These links will get you started, but be warned:

1) It's very easy to spend so long hopping from one site to another that you lose all track of time and end up with none left for practice!

2) Most tabs. (see below) on the internet are reasonably accurate but anyone can post up a tab. so don't assume they are always correct. It is best to buy the official versions published by the artists themselves.

## Guitar Tablature

Before you set off to explore guitar related websites I'd better explain all about guitar tablature (or 'tab.'). This is a short hand alternative to normal music notation. It is very easy to understand and consequently very popular with those who are too lazy to figure out proper music reading. You'll see it used in a lot of guitar books/magazines and also for most of the guitar music on the internet. The rules of tab. are very simple:

1) Tablature uses six lines – one for each guitar string.
2) The numbers written on the string lines show the frets: 1 = 1st fret, 2 = 2nd fret, 0 = open string, etc.
3) If two or more notes are to be played together, they are written on top of one another, just as in standard notation.

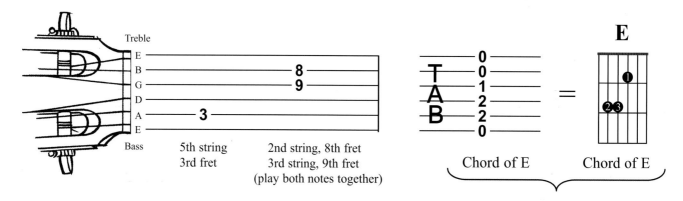

## Chord Notation

Many guitar websites (e.g. www.rawktabs.com) do not show chords in the usual way with chord windows, but indicate the chords instead by a row of six numbers, e.g. 022100 = E. As you've probably guessed, the six numbers represent the frets of the strings, with the numbers on the left being the bass strings. The chord of D, for example, would be shown as: xx0232. An 'x' means that the string is not sounded.

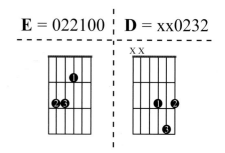

## Rhythm Notation in Tab.

There is usually no indication of note duration or rhythm in tab., the idea being that you already know the rhythm through having heard a recording of the music. Where rhythm is used however, tab. borrows the rhythmic notation of conventional music notation. This is shown in the following tabbed out version of a very well known tune. Have a go at 'tabbing out' the rest of the tune yourself.

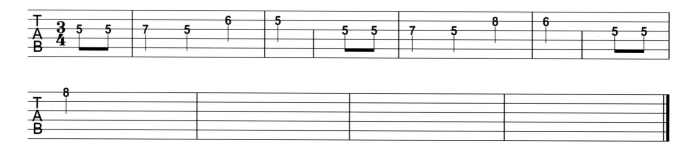

# Homework Diary

**I WANT YOU TO PRACTICE EVERY DAY!**

| C.D Track No. | Page No. | Homework Set | ✓ | ✓ | Date |
|---|---|---|---|---|---|
| 2 | 5 | Amazing Grace | | | |
| 3 | 6 | Omie Wise | | | |
| 4 | 7 | Drunken Sailor | | | |
| 5 | 7 | Country Dance | | | |
| 6 | 7 | Study in G | | | |
| 7 | 9 | Hatikva | | | |
| 8 | 9 | Hava Nagila | | | |
| 9 | 10 | G major Scale | | | |
| 10 | 10 | Troika | | | |
| 11 | 11 | Elegy | | | |
| 12 | 12 | Ma Vlast | | | |
| 13 | 12 | Snake Charmer (bass) | | | |
| 14 | 13 | C major Scale | | | |
| 15 | 13 | A minor Scale | | | |
| 16 | 13 | Twinkle 'by ear' | | | |
| 17 | 14 | Oh, When the Saints | | | |
| 18 | 15 | Boogie Woogie | | | |
| 19 | 15 | Blues scale in G | | | |
| 20 | 15 | 12 bar blues in G | | | |
| 21 | 16 | Strolling Along | | | |
| 22 | 17 | The Music Box | | | |
| 23 | 18 | Heart and Soul | | | |
| 24 | 19 | Go to Sleep | | | |
| | 19 | Another tune 'by ear' | | | |
| 25 | 20 | Daily exercises | | | |
| 26 | 21 | Snake Charmer | | | |
| 27 | 21 | Yankee Doodle | | | |

*Teacher dates and ticks when done*

| 28 | 21 | Together | | | |
|---|---|---|---|---|---|
| | 22 | Correct the mistakes | | | |
| | 22 | Graphic Score | | | |
| 29 | 23 | We Three Kings | | | |
| 30 | 23 | We Three Kings (Bass) | | | |
| 31 | 24 | Asturias | | | |
| 32 | 25 | Danza Española | | | |
| 33 | 26 | The National Anthem | | | |
| 34 | 27 | Auld Lang Syne | | | |
| 35 | 28 | Bluesville | | | |
| 36 | 29 | Greensleeves | | | |
| | 30 | Test! | | | |
| 37 | 31 | Interval Recognition | | | |

## Ensemble & Improvisation

| 38 | 32 | Injuns! | | | |
|---|---|---|---|---|---|
| 39 | 33 | Easy and Sleazy | | | |
| 40 | 34 | Cool Cat Blues | | | |
| 41 | 35 | Long, Long Ago | | | |
| 42 | 36 | Ole | | | |
| 43 | 38 | Pavane | | | |

## Songs & Chord Playing

| 44 | 39 | This Train | | | |
|---|---|---|---|---|---|
| 45 | 40 | Jamaica Farewell | | | |
| 46 | 41 | House of the Rising Sun | | | |
| 47 | 42 | Morning has Broken | | | |
| 48 | 43 | The Sloop John B. | | | |
| | 44 | Transpose Kumbaya | | | |
| | 45 | Chord Test | | | |
| 49 | 45 | Chord Recognition | | | |
| | 46 | Tab. Exercise | | | |

 # Useful Websites

www.guitaracademy.co.uk    Visit my online guitar academy to discover many more useful links, as well as updates and various freebies. You can also buy 'Guitar Academy' books directly from this site, with special discount rates available for teachers.

www.chordfind.com  or  www.all-guitar-chords.com    Visit either of these sites if you need to find a chord.

www.sheetmusicdirect.com    This is the best place to get hold of the official, i.e. 'accurate' tabs. to songs. They currently charge £2.25 per tab. and the artist gets paid a royalty for every download. Highly recommended!

www.e-chords.com    The thing that sets this apart from other tab sites is that as well as showing the chords and lyrics, many of the songs also have a midi accompaniment. You can strum along with the band. Great stuff!

www.geocities.com/eran_talmorg    Download a free metronome to use on your computer. A **metronome** is a useful device that makes a ticking sound that can be adjusted to keep time to the pulse of the music.